# PAINTINGS

P9-BAU-807

Created by Claude Delafosse
and Gallimard Jeunesse
Illustrated by Tony Ross

## A FIRST DISCOVERY **ART** BOOK

Cartwheel
·B·O·O·K·S· ®

SCHOLASTIC INC.
New York   Toronto   London   Auckland   Sydney

The more you study paintings, the more fun
they are to look at.

Michaelangelo takes a rest atop the
scaffolding before painting Adam
on the ceiling of the Sistine Chapel.

What is that strange form rising from the floor?

Look closely at the painting
by Hans Holbein (on the left).

This is a human skull!

Georges de La Tour
painted almost the same
scene twice.

Bruegel the Elder often painted scenes of everyday life in 16th-century Belgium. In *Children's Games*, he painted peasant children at play in a town square.

Study the details of this painting. Do you recognize any of the games the young people are playing?

More than 400 years ago, children played leapfrog, blind man's buff, tag, follow-the-leader, hoops, spinning top, piggyback, hobby-horse — games that look a lot like games we still play today.

Why is Holbein holding that skull?

Skulls in Renaissance paintings were called death's heads.

## See the skull in its normal form. . . .

## Now follow the gradual change as the skull becomes more and more elongated by . . .

anamorphosis

Do you see many differences between the two paintings?

In each of these paintings,
the cheater gets ahead
by hiding an ace
behind his back,
under his belt.

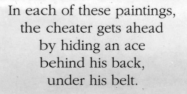

ıs and the rider
ıll dots of color.

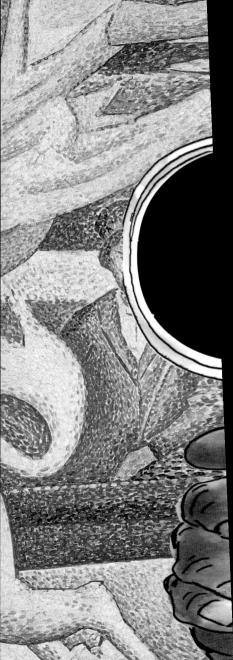

us and the rider
all dots of color.

Turn the transparent page to see ...

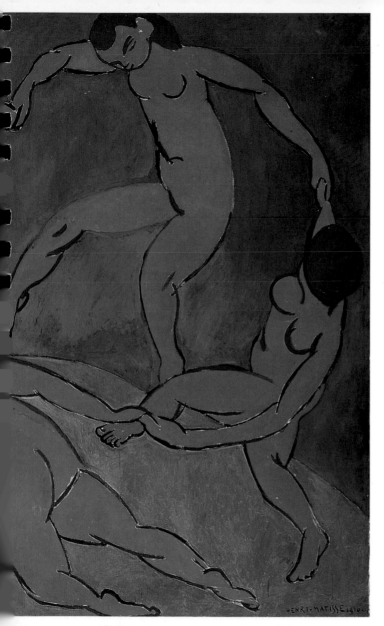

The painting captures the amazing movement of the dancers!

*The Dance*, painted by Henri Matisse.

Let's visit a gallery to see paintings from around the world.

*Snap the Whip*
**Winslow Homer**

*The Magician*
**Hieronymous Bosch**

*A Meeting*
**Marie Bashkirtseff**

*Old Juniet's Carriole*
**Henri Rousseau**

*The Meal*
**Paul Gaugin**

*Children with Lanterns*
**Thadée Makovsky**

*The Dance Class*
**Edgar Degas**

*Three Musicians*
**Pablo Picasso**

Look closely at these details from
the paintings in this book. Can you
tell which paintings they belong to?

Now that you know all these works of art,
why not try to make a painting of your own.

# Table of Illustrations

Cover: **Bruegel the Elder**, *Children's Games* (detail), oil on board, 1560, Kunsthistoriches Museum, Vienna. Photo: E. Lessing/Magnum.

Title page: **Winslow Homer**, *Snap the Whip* (detail), oil on canvas, 1872, The Butler Institute of American Art, Youngstown, Ohio.

**Michaelangelo**, Sistine Chapel ceiling, *The Creation of Adam* (detail), fresco, 1511, The Vatican Museum, Rome. Photo: P. Zigrossi/ A. Bracchetti.

**Hans Holbein the Younger**, *The Ambassadors*, oil on board, 1533, National Gallery, London. Photo: Bridgeman Art Library.

**Bruegel the Elder**, *Children's Games*, oil on board, 1560, Kunsthistoriches Museum, Vienna. Photo: E. Lessing/Magnum.

**Georges de La Tour**, *The Cheat with the Ace of Diamonds*, oil on canvas, ca. late 1620s, Louvre Museum, Paris. Photo: RMN.

**Georges de La Tour**, *The Cheat with the Ace of Clubs*, oil on canvas, late 1620s, Kimbell Art Museum, Fort Worth, Texas.

**Georges Seurat**, *The Circus*, oil on canvas, 1891, Musée d'Orsay, Paris. Photo: RMN.

**Henri Matisse**, *The Dance*, oil on canvas, 1910, The Hermitage, St. Petersberg. Photo and copyright of The Estate of H. Matisse.

**Winslow Homer**, *Snap the Whip*, oil on canvas, 1872, The Butler Institute of American Art, Youngstown, Ohio.

**Hieronymus Bosch**, *The Magician*, oil on board, 1475–1480, Museum of Art and History, Saint-Germain-en-Laye. Photo: Giraudon.

**Marie Bashkirtseff**, *A Meeting*, oil on canvas, 1884, Musée d'Orsay, Paris. Photo: RMN.

**Henri Rousseau**, *Old Juniet's Carriole* (or *Cart*), oil on canvas, 1908, Musée de l'Orangerie, Paris. Photo: RMN.

**Paul Gaugin**, *The Meal*, oil on canvas, 1891, Musée d'Orsay, Paris. Photo: RMN.

**Thadée Makovsky**, *Children with Lanterns*, 1929, National Museum of Modern Art, Paris. Photo: Philippe Migeat/Centre G. Pompidou. D.R.

**Edgar Degas**, *The Dance Class*, oil on canvas, ca. 1873–1876, Musée d'Orsay, Paris. Photo: RMN.

**Pablo Picasso**, *Three Musicians*, oil on canvas, 1921, The Museum of Modern Art, New York. Copyright SPADEM, Paris, 1993.

## Other titles in the *First Discovery Art* series:
Portraits
Landscapes
Animals

*Library of Congress Cataloging-in-Publication Data available.*
Originally published in France under the title *Les Tableaux* by Editions Gallimard.

No part of this publication may be reproduced in whole or in part, or stored in a retrieval system, or transmitted in any form or by any means, electronic, mechanical, photocopying, recording, or otherwise, without written permission of the publisher. For information regarding permission, write to Scholastic Inc., 555 Broadway, New York, NY 10012.

ISBN 0-590-55201-5

Copyright © 1993 by Editions Gallimard. This edition English translation by Pamela Nelson.
This edition Expert Reader: Alice Schwarz, Museum Educator.

All rights reserved. Published by Scholastic Inc., 555 Broadway, New York, NY 10012 by arrangement with Editions Gallimard•Jeunesse, 5 rue Sebastien-Bottin, F-75007, Paris, France.

CARTWHEEL BOOKS and the CARTWHEEL BOOKS logo are registered trademarks of Scholastic Inc.

12 11 10 9 8 7 6 5 4 3 2 1          6 7 8 9/9 0/0

Printed in Italy by Editoriale Libraria

First Scholastic printing, February 1996